Love Letters To My Husband

By Tamara McNair-Hicks J.D.

Dedication

First I have to give honor to God for what He's done in my life; for without Him, I could and would be nothing. This book is dedicated to my loving husband Cavon Hicks and our three children. God has truly blessed me with a wonderful man of God and loving family. To my parents, Thomas and Debra McNair, who never cease to encourage me and push me into my destiny. To my sister Kelly McNair, who always supports my visions, and is down for the cause!

Next, I have to thank one of my best friends, Kimara Glover, who did all my editing and put up with me through it all. To Cedric Wright, Brandy Lovelady-Mitchell, Elizabeth Klein and Dion Thelmas, you each have been a constant source of encouragement, pushing me into all that God calls me to do. Lastly, but not least, to all those who took part in the study; I sincerely want to thank you all, for you have truly been sent by God.

Contents

Love Letters to My Husband

Foreword

In this day and age marriage between a man and a woman seems to be losing its savor. God created man and woman intending that they love each other, become one to procreate and replenish the earth; and such was His intention from the time of the Garden of Eden. Centuries and decades have evolved and man has lost the God-conscious of our creator's purpose and plan for male and female. Even still, God always has a remnant in the earth that will seek to hold fast to His blueprint; one that will endeavor to fulfill His word, and crusade to beseech others to hold fast to His word and promise. God deposits one and calls those who He can trust. One who will walk in spiritual integrity; that lives the life they talk about and will stand for God when no one else will stand with them. One who will endure persecution for the sake of righteousness.

After being married myself for over forty years, I truly understand the endurance and love that it takes to sustain a marriage, and that the key to the success of my marriage was seasoned with three main ingredients: God, love and a mentor who embraced marriage and knew the importance of doing all necessary to maintain the covenant of that marriage. That is why I know *that Tamara McNair Hicks, J.D.* has been called for such a time as this. As a mentor to marriages, I believe that God has given her the wisdom to write the book *"One Love - Love Letters to my Husband."* I have watched her life and seen the love and commitment that she has for God. All of her life she has sought to live righteously, always seeking God to course-correct and direct. Tamara is a person who believes the word of God is true and loves God; constantly striving to apply the principles of God to her life.

Her faithfulness to God has been quintessential, the model that she has and applies to her own marriage, and even when others doubt she holds fast to the covenant she made to her husband. Tamara is a woman walking in spiritual integrity. In her quest to be submitted to her vows and covenant to her spouse, she sought God and He gave her a tool and an innovative and creative way to express her love to her Husband. As she walked in the obedience of God's instruction and stayed faithful to His daily guidance, not only did she find healing for her marriage, but found healing for herself. Having been an eye-witness and a confidant to her I know that this book was written not out of an idea, but out of a submitted heart that has lived out every element of this book without any falsehoods.

***Love Letters to my Husband* written by Tamara McNair Hicks, J.D.** will be a blessing to all married couples that will read and follow the instruction of her teaching. She has been sent as the Mentor to help equip you and your marriage and help root out negative influence. I highly recommend this book to all. I know you will find her to be a great mentor and author who illuminates Godly principles that will strengthen your marriage foundation. My prayer is that millions of marriages will be fortified through these pages and the books to come that are yet being birthed out of her spiritual womb.

Tamara McNair Hicks, J.D., my loving daughter, I love u with all my heart. May the blessings of the Lord chase you down and overtake you.

Evangelist Debra McNair

Mother/Friend/Confidant/Elijah

Love Letters to My Husband

Prologue

I wrote this book in the hopes that many couples who find that they are struggling in their marriages will find a new fervor for God and each other. It's my prayer that this book will reawaken a passion for your husband that may have quieted down through the trials of life and even if you feel your marriage is on track, may it be a tool to stir up that fire, so it burns brighter. I want to see you blessed and walking in the full potential of your marriage. It is my sincerest desire that this book gives you a deeper understanding of God's love and that you will seek out how to love God through his word, that it will ignite a new passion in you for Him, and in turn that same desire will catapult you into a new relationship with your husband.

When I went through this 30 day process I was already a licensed minister and a believer in Christ, but I have found that every day with God is new and we should approach the word of God this way. As you experience His word, let it permeate and resonate in your spirit. Really think and meditate on the scriptures before you begin writing your letter to your spouse, let God show you His love and then after you have gotten the revelation, and once that revelation ignites in you, apply that same revelation to your spouse. If you have yet to find Christ it is impossible to know love for the Bible says, "thy God is love" (1 John 4:8). I urge you to take the time and accept Him into your life, prior to this exercise, so that you can truly be open to the leading of the Holy Spirit.

My letters are just a template for you to follow, please don't try and replicate my style or spend too much time comparing your letters to mine. Please use your own way of expressing your love to your spouse. This will make it an intimate experience that only you two will share. I kept all 30 hand-written letters to my husband, some of the letters in this book had to be altered just a little, others you will read are exact, but overall the integrity of what was said has been maintained.

Love Letters to My Husband

I can't express how important it is that you do the exercises in this book. Take the time to write your feelings so that you have a real understanding of how you change, as well as how your spouse is changing. The most important thing that I learned is to make the time. Often we don't take the time where it counts. Don't get so busy with the jobs, family, children or church that you neglect your covenant with your spouse. Have fun and be creative. Use pet names! Be seductive or just be sincere. Whatever your style, try to keep them guessing about what you will say next. I'm looking forward to your own testimonies and victories, which only God can bring to our marriages.

I pray sincerely that this book will do what it needs to do in your life. That you will be enriched and blessed and that the love of Jesus will work a miracle on your behalf, for we know all things are possible through Christ (Matthew 10:27).

Love Letters to My Husband

Introduction

I got married on August 16, 2008. I was 31 years old and after much prayer, fasting, waiting and hoping, God allowed a wonderful man to enter into my life. I was sure marriage would be a challenge, but I thought that at least we would have a few years before the challenging times hit. Little did I know that the "honeymoon period" is more of a fallacy than a reality, especially when you're trying to meld two very different lives into "one".

I am going to talk a little about the problems my husband and I faced and how after I was done trying it "my way," the King of Kings stepped in and made a change in my marriage. What I could not do for myself in 31 years, took God only a mere 30 days.

I was a single young woman in law school when I finally met my husband. At that point in time I had decided that if God wanted me to be married, then He would have to send somebody to me. While I couldn't wait to be married, I was tired of "dating." I had *almost* been engaged twice before and both experiences ended in failure (and I'm talking EPIC failure, the magnitude of which is truly a story in itself, but I digress). I was going to school full time and had sworn off men. It just so happened that I was still a member of the social media website Myspace and checked my account quite regularly, more so out of habit, than hope. Just when I least expected it, God showed up and there appeared a handsome fellow on my web page, claiming to know me from somewhere. After a four-month courtship, he popped the question and so began our journey!

Love Letters to My Husband

The Marriage

Married life is different for everyone. We all have preconceived ideas of what marriage will be like and many times we are disillusioned by the false impressions that are set in our minds by our various surroundings. We receive images from the media, our family, and friends. We see pictures of the perfect family that we have always wanted or the residue of the battered and torn relationships that we have grown up in. Both of these images can lead us into a place of discontentment.

We become disillusioned when our own marriages fail to reflect the images that we grew up with. Some of us had wonderful family lives and assume that the person we are marrying understands the dichotomy of marriage as we do. Then there are others for whom a broken family life was the norm, and who have a hard time operating outside of the dysfunction in which they have become accustomed. Either way, when we marry our spirits become one, but our flesh is screaming and kicking against this concept!

We all have so many preconceptions, this makes things tricky, because they become the standard of which we live out and fulfill our lives. So whether you have had a broken/dysfunctional home or a vision of perfection, you either embrace this same mind set or you run from it with all your might, thereby erecting a false sense of family in your mind that can shatter your marital life. The question you have to ask yourself is: Am I willing to give up these ideas for the sake of my marriage, or will I hold onto these concepts no matter what the cost?

Love Letters to My Husband

The Honey Moon Phase

For most marriages starting out, people will tell you that there is a honeymoon phase. This phase is likened to a fairy tale where everything is wonderful and happy. Your prince charming comes to take you into his arms and the two of you ride off into the sunset "happily ever after". Maybe this happened for some of you, but for me this phase didn't exist! When *I* got married, it was a battle! When our *actual* honeymoon was over (I mean literally, when we flew home from Jamaica), so too, was our *metaphorical* honeymoon...Over.

Think of this concept logically: you are taking two very different lives, with different upbringings and attempting to merge them together as one. Doesn't that sound **hard** to you? In my experience, it was more like a battle of wills. Who will conquer? Who will stand on top and like a gladiator be the victor? What kind of honeymoon is that?

Let me be clear, in our marriage, we have had good times and bad times, but I learned that only Jehovah would be able to transform our minds to make the necessary switch to becoming one. The Bible states in Romans 12:2, "and be not conformed to this world, but be ye transformed by the renewing of your minds."

We needed to make the switch from being separate entities, to married people. Believe me, reaching that state proved to be harder than I thought. I predicted how my marriage would be in my mind, but it never dawned on me that I was marrying a man that had his own ideas about wedded bliss. We started out seemingly on one accord, and then before I could get my wedding dress put away, trouble erupted in the Hicks home.

Love Letters to My Husband

Trouble in the Land

I want to give you the short and quick of my story. Later, in another book, I'll go into more detail, but for now, I'll give just a glimpse of all we were going through. The first year of my marriage went something like this:

We got married. We got pregnant. My new husband came with an adolescent son from a previous marriage, who could be really challenging to say the least. I was struggling with instant motherhood and according to my husband, I was the cure for every issue (past or present) that arose with our son. There were family members that were against us, and were real negative influences to our relationship; and because I was a full-time graduate student, on top of everything else, money was tight. Imagine it, all of this strife, before we could even reach our first anniversary.

Needless to say, I came to a place where I felt like I had made a mistake. I thought, 'maybe I hadn't heard God correctly'. I wondered how so much could be going wrong already. I didn't understand. I was confused. I knew that I had asked God about this man, and I was certain He showed me this man as my husband, but nothing was going right. I was fed up and tired. All I could think was, 'God if you don't fix this marriage, then I can't see spending years in all this chaos!'

Love Letters to My Husband

God Answered Me

Yes, God answers our prayers. Although, not always in the way we think He will, because I was expecting God to *get* my husband. I mean, wear him out! Bring the pain! Show him what was what. I was really expecting Him to show my husband the error in his ways, *because you know I was right*! It was *he* who was doing all these things to *me.* I was innocent!

Instead, God showed me myself, and He reminded me of the commitment I had made to my marriage. He told me that He wanted to teach me something. I thought, 'so, You're not going to get him God?' He said 'no, I want to teach you something, and it will take you 30 days to accomplish it.'

I was flabbergasted, what could I possibly do in 30 days to correct any of the things that was wrong with my marriage? He told me of a love story, how He loved me, even when I was unlovable. He said, 'if you go down this journey with me, it will be transforming to you and your marriage.' First He told me that I had to write my husband a love letter every day for 30 days. Now, I wasn't too happy about that since I wasn't feeling the love at this point. I was just mad.

 Secondly, He told me that I had to use scripture from the Bible about love <u>only.</u> Thirdly, in the letters, I could not tell my husband what he was doing wrong; I could only tell him what I would do for him according to the scriptures that God would give me. I had to make a thirty day commitment and I could not waiver, even if he made me mad during the process. I had to write the letters and discuss them with him at night, he could then tell me what he would do according to the scripture, but he was not required to do so. This began my journey to finding out how to love God, and in turn how to love my husband.

Love Letters to My Husband

The Journey

I will give you some examples of the letters that I wrote to my husband. I do not want you to copy them. They are just to get you started. Every marriage is uniquely different and personal. God wants to share with you, what to write and what to say. The only way this is going to be beneficial to your marriage is to open up your heart and pour out what you think and feel.

Remember that you are to write a letter from the standpoint of what you would do for your spouse according to scripture (not what you want or think they should be doing for you).

Chapter 1 - The Beginning
Days 1 Through 7

Love Letters to My Husband

Love Letters to My Husband

DAY 1

"For this reason a man will leave his father and mother and be united to his wife and they will become one flesh."

The letter... This is what I wrote to my husband, you can use it as a template. My Husband's pet name is Honey Bear. Make it endearing and personal; find terms that only you two will share.

Dear love (Honey Bear),

*Last night as I listened to your heart beat and it synced with mine, it reminded me that we are one flesh. So when you struggle, I struggle, when you hurt, I hurt and when you experience pain I feel it as well. At the same time I also experience joy and laughter, your success and failures. That's when I am reminded that **together** we can do the impossible, reach the highest mountain peaks and soar to great heights. I love you, be encouraged today and know that we are one, mind, body, and spirit.*

Now it's your turn, you will find a work page to help you on your journey!

Love Letters to My Husband

Day 1

Scripture: Genesis 2:24

NIV: For this reason a man will leave his father and mother and be united to his wife, and they will become one flesh.

Focus: When writing this letter I focused on the words one flesh. This is not the only focus, allow the Holy Spirit to lead you in what your focus will be.

_____

_____

_____

_____

_____

_____

_____

_____

_____

_____

Use the above to write your letter. Remember that you are telling your husband what you will do according to the scriptures, not what he needs to do for you! This can be difficult, but the exercise is in you finding your place in the relationship.

Next... Discuss the scripture with your spouse during the day or at night (basically your free quiet time together. Please make time, this is important). Also ask for his reflection as to his role. What can he do to follow the scripture towards you? Now use this space to journal: What was the outcome?

_____

_____

_____

_____

_____

Please don't be discouraged if you are not getting the response that you want from your husband, this is only day 1.

Love Letters to My Husband

"Jacob was in love with Rachel and said, "I'll work for you seven years in return for your younger daughter Rachel.""

The letter... What stood out to me about this passage was the word Work. We have to work at our marriages and so I wrote my letter from this standpoint. Remember the letters are to be personal, so feel free to write from your own point of view.

> *(Honey Bear),*
>
> *Sometimes we have to work for love and at love. I am willing to work for our relationship even when times get rough, when I don't understand and when I'm angry. I will remember the vows you wrote especially for me and what I wrote for you. Those vows remind me of the commitment I made to do whatever it takes to make our marriage work. I waited much, much longer than seven years for God to send me you so I can make the sacrifice like Jacob, of my time and energy to choose us always.*

Now it's your turn, you will find a work page to help you on your journey!

Love Letters to My Husband

Day 2

Scripture: Genesis 29:18

NIV: "Jacob was in love with Rachel and said, "I'll work for you seven years in return for your younger daughter Rachel.""

Focus: When writing this letter I focused on the word 'work' and what I was willing to do for my spouse. This is not the only focus; allow God to lead you to your proper focus.

_____
_____
_____
_____
_____
_____
_____
_____
_____
_____
_____
_____

Use the above to write your letter. Remember that you are telling your husband what you will do according to the scriptures, not what he needs to do for you!

Next... Discuss the scripture with your spouse during the day or at night (basically your free quiet time together, please make time, this **is important**). Also ask for his reflection as to his role. What can he do to follow the scripture towards you?

What was the outcome?

_____
_____
_____
_____
_____

It is important to stick with the process. Keep in mind what you want God to do in your marriage.

Love Letters to My Husband

"A new command I give you: Love one another; as I have loved you, so you must love one another."

The letter... What stood out to me about this passage was Commandment. We have to love one another as God loves us. That was a deep revelation for me and so I wrote my letter from this standpoint.

Dear Heart,

When I think about how God loves me. He loves me through the good and the bad, the times that I listened and when I didn't. He loved me when I yelled and screamed and when I was soft and kind. When I was doing my thing (sinning) and when I repented and lived holy. Through it all God loved me. So I pledge to love you, when we agree or not, scream or talk, cry or laugh, act right or wrong. I love you because God loved me enough not to give up so I choose to love you and know that through it all we are one.

Now it's your turn, will find a work page to help you on your journey!

Love Letters to My Husband

Day 3

Scripture: John 13:34

NIV: "A new command I give you: Love one another; as I have loved you, so you must love one another."

Focus: My focus was on the commandment to love as God loves us. This does not have to be your focus, let the Holy Spirit lead you to write what's best for your spouse.

_____
_____
_____
_____
_____
_____
_____
_____
_____
_____
_____

Use the above to write your letter. Remember that you are telling your husband what you will do according to the scriptures, not what he needs to do for you!

Next... Discuss the scripture with your spouse during the day or at night (basically your free quiet time together, please make time this is important). Also ask for his reflection as to his role. What can he do to follow the scripture towards you?

What was the outcome?

_____
_____
_____
_____
_____

Did you have a challenging day with your spouse? Don't get discouraged; day 30 will be here before you know it!

Day 4

"Many waters cannot quench love; rivers cannot wash it away. If one were to give all the wealth of his house for love, it would be utterly scorned."

The letter… What stood out to me about this passage was how strong God's love is for us. Material possessions cannot replace God's love. When you really meditate on this scripture, it gives you just a glimpse of the Father's heart and how we should in turn love our spouses with this same deep, penetrating love.

Dearest Love of My Life,

I thank God for his love towards us, and the fact that nothing was greater than his love. He loved the world so much that he laid down his life for it. I know that nothing can replace true love and as I live my life with you, it is my prayer that our love grows as strong a God's love for us. I know for sure that money, jewelry, clothing or any material thing cannot replace my love for you. So, I offer you my love and I make this commitment, I will work diligently to strengthen our bond so that I will be able to stand strong and say that many waters cannot quench my love for you.

Now it's your turn, you will find a work page to help you on your journey!

Love Letters to My Husband

Day 4

Scripture: Song of Songs 8:7

NIV: "Many waters cannot quench love; rivers cannot wash it away. If one were to give all the wealth of his house for love, it would be utterly scorned."

Focus: I focused on strength this helped me to write my letter. What will your focus be? Let the Holy Spirit guide you.

_____

_____

_____

_____

_____

_____

_____

_____

_____

_____

Use the above to write your letter. Remember that you are telling your husband what you will do according to the scriptures, not what he needs to do for you! This can be difficult but the exercise is in you finding your place in the relationship.

Next... Discuss the scripture with your spouse during the day or at night (basically your free quiet time together, please make time this is important). Also ask for his reflection as to his role. What can he do to follow the scripture towards you?

What was the outcome?

_____

_____

_____

_____

_____

This is a good time to start seeking God for the changes you want to see in your marriage and in yourself. Keep in mind that this journey is one of self-discovery.

Day 5

"Husbands love your wives, just as Christ loved the church and gave himself up for her. [26]to make her holy, cleansing her by the washing with water through the word."

The letter... What stood out to me about this passage was God's love for the church and how he gave himself for it. Then it hit me how He purified us by His blood and the word of God. How awesome it is to have a godly man. Note that if your spouse is unsaved, you can keep in mind that when writing this letter how you will love him through the word of god. The Bible says the unbelieving spouse is sanctified through the believing spouse.

My Husband,

When I think about how you pray for me, and how hard you work to take care of me, it makes me that much more grateful for you. When I see you attend church and how you have a sincere desire to be a great man of God, both in the natural and spiritual, it encourages me to want to be better. I thank God for having a man that will cover me and put Christ first. So I will make every effort to support you in your endeavors, listen to your counsel and work hard to make sure that I stay in my proper place in our relationship. I love you

Now it's your turn, you will find a work page to help you on your journey!

Love Letters to My Husband

Day 5

Scripture: Ephesians 5:25-26

NIV: "Husbands love your wives, just as Christ loved the church and gave himself up for her. [26]to make her holy, cleansing her by the washing with water through the word."

Focus: There is wealth of revelation in this scripture! Take your time and remember if you want to see change, see it in yourself first, and then speak it into existence.

_____
_____
_____
_____
_____
_____
_____
_____
_____
_____

Use the above to write your letter. Remember that you are telling your husband what you will do according to the scriptures, not what he needs to do for you! This can be difficult but the exercise is in you finding your place in the relationship.

Next... Discuss the scripture with your spouse during the day or at night (basically your free quiet time together, please make time this is important). Also ask for his reflection as to his role. What can he do to follow the scripture towards you?

What was the outcome?

_____
_____
_____
_____
_____

Habakkuk 2:2 says to write the vision and make it plain that he make run that reads it...Keep your eye on the prize and your mind stayed on the outcome!

Love Letters to My Husband

"In this same way, husbands ought to love their wives as their own bodies. He who loves his wife loves himself. [29]After all, no one ever hated his own body, but he feeds and cares for it, just as Christ does the church."

The letter... The human body is a mystery; in order to survive we must take care of it. Oh, how we will groom and take care of our bodies to make sure that we are presentable to others! We should do at least that much when caring for our spouse. Make sure you find your own focus, and continue to let the Holy Spirit lead you.

My Husband,

As I watch you groom yourself, exercise (when u can) wash and cleanse your body, cut your hair, take pride in your appearance, and overall make sure you have nourishment for your body. I think wow, he is going to care for me the way he cares for himself, and then I can't help but to be grateful. As I think on the things you have done for me, the rubbing of my feet, the rest when I'm tired and handing over the paycheck. I am thankful. I ask God to let me grow strong in him, so the way I think, feel and act is a mirror image of the one who created me. I declare the fruits of the spirit will come forth in me, so that when I am loving you, I am loving you the way I love myself and the way God intended.

Now it's your turn, you will find a work page to help you on your journey!

Love Letters to My Husband

Day 6

Scripture: Ephesians 5:28-29

NIV: "In this same way, husbands ought to love their wives as their own bodies. He who loves his wife loves himself. [29]After all, no one ever hated his own body, but he feeds and cares for it, just as Christ does the church."

Focus: What would you do if you had to love someone the way you loved yourself? I wouldn't let anyone take my life I'd fight for it. What is your focus?

_____
_____
_____
_____
_____
_____
_____
_____
_____

Use the above to write your letter. Remember that you are telling your husband what you will do according to the scriptures, not what he needs to do for you! This can be difficult but the exercise is in you finding your place in the relationship.

Next... Discuss the scripture with your spouse during the day or at night (basically your free quiet time together, please make time this is important). Also ask for his reflection as to his role. What can he do to follow the scripture towards you?

What was the outcome?

_____
_____
_____
_____
_____

Would you fight for your life? Then you should fight just as hard for your marriage. Keep pressing for the promise!

Day 7

"Because your love is better than life, my lips will glorify you"

The letter... I focused on the words 'better than life'. Life is fleeting and only lasts but a moment, but God's love is eternal, never ending, all sustaining and it will never pass away. Oh how I glorify my Father in heaven! What is your focus? There is so much revelation in God's word.

My Sweetie Face,

Today, I think about how God has allowed us to share our lives together, I ponder on how short and fleeting life can be. It makes me happy to know that God has allowed us to spend this life together. I will love you with my whole heart. I will love you beyond time, through this life and into the next. Life is short, so I won't take for granted the time we have together, I won't let anger, a disagreement or an argument fester until the morning. It is my goal to never waste time in anger but to forgive quickly and spend as much of my time in love and loving you. I want you to say to me that my love has been better than life.

Now it's your turn, you will find a work page to help you on your journey!

Love Letters to My Husband

Day 7

Scripture: Psalms 63:3

NIV: "Because your love is better than life, my lips will glorify you."

Focus: What could you do to make your love for your spouse better than life? This was my focus, what is yours?

_____

_____

_____

_____

_____

_____

_____

_____

_____

Use the above to write your letter. Remember that you are telling your husband what you will do according to the scriptures, not what he needs to do for you! Life is an awesome gift given to all of us, think of your best moments, now how would you top that?

Next... Discuss the scripture with your spouse during the day or at night (basically your free quiet time together, please make time this is important). Also ask for his reflection as to his role. What can he do to follow the scripture towards you?

What was the outcome?

_____

_____

_____

_____

Thoughts for Week 1

This week I was feeling – Anxious

I was really feeling nervous about the whole project, my thoughts centered around Is my husband going to respond to the process? Is he going to talk with me about the letter? Is he truly receiving the letters, the way I intended him to? He was agreeable to do the process, we talked about the letters, and he didn't have much to say about how he could apply the letters towards me. But it was a start that we were even able to discuss them. O.K Lord now, you got me doing a lot, I hope this works!

How do you feel after this week?

_____
_____
_____
_____
_____
_____
_____
_____
_____
_____
_____
_____
_____
_____
_____

When doing these exercises it's important to keep in mind that you are being transformed by the renewing of your mind. Pray today that God changes you and makes you the woman your spouse needs.

Chapter 2 - Keep Moving
Days 8 Through 14

Love Letters to My Husband

"From him the whole body, joined and held together by every supporting ligament, grows and builds itself up in love, as each part does its work."

The letter… I love this particular passage of scripture. God gave this to me specifically to teach me the inner workings of the body of Christ. This is the model to follow for the family. There is no me without my husband, we both have strengths and weaknesses but, if we cover the weaknesses with love and allow our individual strengths to combine we will be an unstoppable force.

My Husband,

Last night, and truthfully many other nights I became discouraged with our relationship. My feelings were hurt and I was angry, after a while I was just hurt. I thought about how I did not like your response, when I asked you to get up at night to do something for me or get something for the baby. I was tempted to hold on to the anger, but God showed me how many times he has asked of us to do something and our response has been "I'm Tired," "I don't feel like it" or we have done things for him begrudgingly. Today I thank God for revelation that the body works by each individual part functioning together and providing the necessary support so things can work the way they need to. I am encouraged today that even if your reaction is not what I am looking for, without the support you do give me with our daughter and your individual role as well, we would crumble or fall apart. So I will do my part in love. And I know you do yours in love, and I won't complain.

Love your wife

Now it's your turn, you will find a work page to help you on your journey!

Love Letters to My Husband

Day 8

Scripture: Ephesians 4:16

> **NIV:** "From him the whole body, joined and held together by every supporting ligament, grows and builds itself up in love, as each part does its work."

Focus: What can you do, to make your marriage function more effectively, is it forgiveness or something else?

_____
_____
_____
_____
_____
_____
_____
_____
_____
_____
_____
_____

Use the above to write your letter. Remember that you are telling your husband what you will do according to the scriptures, not what he needs to do for you! This can be difficult but the exercise is in you finding your place in the relationship.

Next... Discuss the scripture with your spouse during the day or at night (basically your free quiet time together, please make time this is important). Also ask for his reflection as to his role. What can he do to follow the scripture towards you?

What was the outcome?

_____
_____
_____
_____
_____

Keep pushing forward in these exercises, try not to dwell on what is not happening, but what is God teaching you about his love.

Day 9

"But God demonstrates his own love for us in this: While we were still sinners, Christ died for us"

The letter... This scripture reminds me of the importance of not only saying verbally I LOVE YOU, but the importance of DEMONSTRATING that love.

My Husband,

As your wife, I think about what you need from me, and I do my very best to show you love from my heart. Sometimes we have an idea of what we think shows our spouses love, but it's more important to understand what (you) consider ways that I can love you. So I will listen to you and take note, so I can show you love in the way that you understand it. I try to show you love by taking care of our home, children, cooking and spending time with you. Today I want you to think of ways I can show you love from your perspective and I we will discuss it tonight.

Love your wife

Now it's your turn, you will find a work page to help you on your journey!

Love Letters to My Husband

Day 9

Scripture: Romans 5:8

NIV: But God demonstrates his own love for us in this: While we were still sinners, Christ died for us.

Focus: You can use my example, or one of your own. This scripture can also speak to God dying for us, even when we were not perfect

_____
_____
_____
_____
_____
_____
_____
_____
_____
_____
_____
_____

Use the above space to write your letter. Remember that you are telling your husband what you will do according to the scriptures, not what he needs to do for you! This can be difficult but the exercise is in you finding your place in the relationship.

Next... Discuss the scripture with your spouse during the day or at night (basically your free quiet time together, please make time this is important). Also ask for his reflection as to his role. What can he do to follow the scripture towards you?

What was the outcome?

_____
_____
_____
_____
_____

As we focus on what God wants to change in us, we will see a change in our spouses.

Love Letters to My Husband

"Husbands, love your wives and do not be harsh with them."

The letter… This scripture reminds me how God will correct us in love, but more than that, I am reminded that how God sees our tears and takes count of every one.

My Husband,

I know that you see the strong side of me and I know that my strength seems unbreakable. God reminds me that he made me the weaker vessel; tender, kind, full of emotion and even frail. I have been strong most of my life, because most times outside of my father there has been no other man around to take care of me. My Strength is a mechanism that developed in me for survival, to keep my feeling from being hurt, to keep me moving forward, and from having to rely on anyone but God. But when he gave me you, he is teaching me how to let you lead, that I don't always have to be strong. I am reminded that when we are in disagreement a soft word turns away wrath. I am the weaker vessel, I need patience and I will remember that when I am speaking to you.

Love your wife

Now it's your turn, you will find a work page to help you on your journey!

Love Letters to My Husband

Day 10

Scripture: Colossians 3:19

NIV: Husbands, love your wives and do not be harsh with them.

Focus: This is a difficult passage to use, you may be tempted to bash you husband with it but resist the devil and he will flee from you! Discuss the way this can work towards you husband.

_____
_____
_____
_____
_____
_____
_____
_____
_____
_____
_____
_____

Use the above to write your letter. Remember that you are telling your husband what you will do according to the scriptures, not what he needs to do for you! This can be difficult but the exercise is in you finding your place in the relationship.

Next... Discuss the scripture with your spouse during the day or at night (basically your free quiet time together, please make time this is important). Also ask for his reflection as to his role. What can he do to follow the scripture towards you?

What was the outcome?

_____
_____
_____
_____
_____

Please don't be discouraged if you are not getting the response that you want from your husband. Keep moving forward.

Love Letters to My Husband

"The reason my Father loves me is that I lay down my life—only to take it up again."

The letter... What stands out for me in this scripture is the fact that the Savior willingly laid down His life and in doing so found favor with God. No one could take His life; He had to willingly lay it down.

Dear Heart,

I have to willingly give my will over to my husband. My commitment to you supersedes the commitments I have made to other people including myself (except God) but I must willingly give my will, my submission, and my power. Because our marriage comes first, so I am committing to you. I choose us above all else, because I know it pleases God. I want us to come together and be in God's full, perfect will. Even if that means giving up something that I want so we can meet our family goals and needs.

Love your wifey,

This was hard to write, I mean hard-hard, I am a very strong woman, but God showed me strength in submission. I said ***ouch*** just typing it!

Now it's your turn, you will find a work page to help you on your journey!

Love Letters to My Husband

Day 11

Scripture: John 10:17

NIV: The reason my Father loves me is that I lay down my life—only to take it up again.

Focus: What will you lay down or give up for your spouse? Are you dedicated to something (job, hobby, etc.) that you are putting above your family?

_____
_____
_____
_____
_____
_____
_____
_____
_____
_____
_____
_____
_____

Use the above to write your letter. Remember that you are telling your husband what you will do according to the scriptures, not what he needs to do for you! This can be difficult but the exercise is in you finding your place in the relationship.

Next... Discuss the scripture with your spouse during the day or at night (basically your free quiet time together, please make time this is important). Also ask for his reflection as to his role. What can he do to follow the scripture towards you?

What was the outcome?

_____
_____
_____
_____
_____

Please don't be discouraged you are making progress, if not in the natural, definitely in the spirit.

Day 12

"For He is gracious and compassionate, slow to anger and abounding in love,
and he relents from sending calamity."

The letter... I sincerely believe this should be the marriage National Anthem or slogan. When I think about how God's wrath has been held back from me, even when I know I was doing wrong, it truly helps me think about my marriage.

> *Dear Heart,*
>
> *I think about my quick temper sometimes and even more my quick tongue, and it makes me stop and think that I can't always take things personally. We all have bad days, and that's not to say that we don't need to change, but we have to give each other some leeway. There are a thousand things that can make me mad during the course of a week, (but) is it really worth being angry about them? Just like God has forgiven us and had grace for us. I have to have grace for you and not expect you to change overnight. How much more would I enjoy my husband, my marriage, my family, if I would take on God's view point! I love you and I know you love me, but it's God that does the changing; and while I am waiting for the change, I will love you in spite of it all. Be slow to anger and abound in love.*
>
> *Love your baby doll,*

Now it's your turn, you will find a work page to help you on your journey!

Love Letters to My Husband

Day 12

Scripture: Joel 2:13

NIV: For He is gracious and compassionate, slow to anger and abounding in love, and he relents from sending calamity.

Focus: What will you choose as your focus based on this passage? Do you need to check your love level? *See: light hearted love level test at the back of the book*

_____

_____

_____

_____

_____

_____

_____

_____

_____

_____

_____

_____

Use the above space to write your letter. Remember that you are telling your husband what you will do according to the scriptures, not what he needs to do for you! This can be difficult but the exercise is in you finding your place in the relationship.

Next... Discuss the scripture with your spouse during the day or at night (basically your free quiet time together, please make time this is important). Also ask for his reflection as to his role. What can he do to follow the scripture towards you?

What was the outcome?

_____

_____

_____

_____

_____

Begin to declare the promises of God over your marriage and your home. Declare you will see a change.

Day 13

"We remember before our God and Father your work produced by faith, your labor prompted by love, and your endurance inspired by hope in our Lord Jesus Christ."

The letter… My focus is actually on a specific portion of this scripture "labor of love", this is significant to me because immediately it brought to mind Labor pains!

Dear Heart,

When I think back to the birth of our child, I think about all that my body went through in the preparation of her birth. The contractions, my water breaking, dilation of my cervix, and the pushing, etc. My body went through great changes and often great pain to deliver our precious child. So it makes me see that a great sacrifice and great pain is sometimes needed to have great love. We will experience great change (we will labor) and it won't always feel good, but it is necessary to have great love. So I will labor to birth out the gift that God has given me... Because you're worth it ...I Love you.

Wifey,

Now it's your turn, you will find a work page to help you on your journey!

Love Letters to My Husband

Day 13

Scripture: 1 Thessalonians 1:3

NIV: We remember before our God and Father your work produced by faith, your labor prompted by love, and your endurance inspired by hope in our Lord Jesus Christ

Focus: What will you choose?

_____
_____
_____
_____
_____
_____
_____
_____
_____
_____
_____
_____

Use the above to write your letter. Remember that you are telling your husband what you will do according to the scriptures, not what he needs to do for you! This can be difficult but the exercise is in you finding your place in the relationship.

Next... Discuss the scripture with your spouse during the day or at night (basically your free quiet time together, please make time this is important). Also ask for his reflection as to his role. What can he do to follow the scripture towards you?

What was the outcome?

_____
_____
_____
_____
_____

Keep declaring by faith over your marriage; declare the changes that you want to see, and watch them happen.

Day 14

*"Let him kiss me with the kisses of his mouth for your love is more
delightful than wine.
3Pleasing is the fragrance of your perfumes; your name is like perfume
poured out.
No wonder the young women love you! 4Take me away with you let us
hurry! Let the king bring me into his chambers."*

The letter... This passage reminds me of new love. The first time we met,
our first kiss and our honey moon. I remember how we prayed that we
never lose these feelings for each other. I focused the beauty of this love.

Baby,

*This passage talks about how your love is better than wine. When
you think about wine you cannot ignore its intoxicating properties,
it can put you in a false state of mind. You can lose your inhibitions
and do things you wouldn't normally do. Well baby, the love we
have goes way beyond that intoxicating feeling. It helps me focus,
it enriches my life and it empowers me to go forward into my
dreams, goals and destiny. I am willing to enrich you, love you and
push you into your God given pursuits and always remember to
love you like the first day we met.*

Now it's your turn, you will find a work page to help you on your journey!

Love Letters to My Husband

Day 14

Scripture: Song of Songs 1:2-4

NIV: Let him kiss me with the kisses of his mouth for your love is more delightful than wine.[3] Pleasing is the fragrance of your perfumes; your name is like perfume poured out. No wonder the young women love you! [4]Take me away with you let us hurry! Let the king bring me into his chambers.

Focus: You can take the approach you want to take, you can use any or all of it to express your love.

_____
_____
_____
_____
_____
_____
_____
_____
_____
_____

Use the above to write your letter. Remember that you are telling your husband what you will do according to the scriptures, not what he needs to do for you! This can be difficult but the exercise is in you finding your place in the relationship.

Next... Discuss the scripture with your spouse during the day or at night (basically your free quiet time together, please make time this is important). Also ask for his reflection as to his role. What can he do to follow the scripture towards you?

What was the outcome?

_____
_____
_____
_____
_____

Feeling like you want to quit? Please push through; this is a good point to start taking inventory.

Thoughts for Week 2

This week I was feeling –upset

I was feeling upset after the weekend visit with my son, we had a falling out, so it was really hard to write this week and be positive. I'm praying God will help me push through and that my anger will not come out in my letters. This is harder than I thought; can I just be sarcastic a little?

How do you feel after this week?

_____

_____

_____

_____

_____

_____

_____

_____

_____

_____

_____

_____

_____

_____

_____

_____

_____

_____

_____

Day 15

"For God so loved the world that he gave his one and only Son, that whoever believes in him shall not perish but have eternal life."

The letter... This letter is the epitome of God's love for us, and so I am focusing on sacrificial love. God gave the ultimate sacrifice for us...What will I sacrifice for my marriage, for my husband?

> Honey Bear,
>
> Love equals sacrifice and the sacrifice of some of the most precious things that we hold dear. God was willing to give up His very son, so that we might have life. It makes me think about what I am willing to give up for you and our marriage. We truly have to be selfless, even Hannah gave her son back to God, and for that He blessed her. It is my sincerest prayer that we will love each other the way Christ loved the church. I am willing to sacrifice my comforts, my sleep, my hobbies, my time, my money and much more, to ensure that our marriage is everything that God wants it to be. I truly love you
>
> Love you,
>
> ME

Now it's your turn, you will find a work page to help you on your journey!

Love Letters to My Husband

Day 15

Scripture: John 3:16

NIV: For God so loved the world that he gave his one and only Son, that whoever believes in him shall not perish but have eternal life.

Focus: Now read the scripture carefully ask the Holy Spirit for His leading when choosing what part of the scripture to focus on. You can do it!

_____
_____
_____
_____
_____
_____
_____
_____
_____
_____
_____
_____

Use the space above to write your letter. Remember that you are telling your husband what you will do according to the scriptures, not what he needs to do for you! This can be difficult but the exercise is in you finding your place in the relationship.

Next... Discuss the scripture with your spouse during the day or at night (basically your free quiet time together, please make this time a priority, it is important). Also ask for his reflection as to his role. What can he do to follow the scripture towards you?

What was the outcome?

_____
_____
_____
_____
_____

Love Letters to My Husband

The Halfway Point

At this point you may be feeling as if things are going fabulously, or they are not changing at all. However let me encourage you to keep moving forward. In Habakkuk 2:2 it tells us to write the vision and make it plain. So I encourage you today to write out the changes that you want to see in your marriage and began to pray over them every day. Also, the Bible talks of declaring a thing, Job 22:28 says to "declare a thing and let it be established unto you". So speak over your marriage, not just any random thing, but the word of God. I will post below some scriptures that you can use to declare the work of God over you marriage daily.

During this point in time, I was really beginning to understand the word of the Lord concerning my marriage. You will see how my letters change, I began to espouse the lesson God gave me and then talk to my husband in those terms. My letters are just a template for you to follow, but please make it personal. Actually at day 15, we had a disagreement and I was ready to give up, but the word was becoming alive to me, and I knew it was the enemy trying to stop our progress, so I pushed forward. I truly thought about how God loved me when I was unlovable, when I was not doing everything right, but he pushed through to love me into the kingdom. Our relationship was showing progress, baby steps, we were talking more, he appreciated the letters, he was surprised by the content and that I felt that type of love for him. You have to celebrate every change that you see, even small victories, turn into bigger victories. So I encourage you to push forward. Here are some things to declare over your marriage, these are what I used, maybe some of them will be helpful to you (see back of book for Declarations).

Love Letters to My Husband

This is the halfway point, the perfect time to reflect and celebrate changes in your marriage up to this point. Surprise your spouse with a "love gift" make sure it's thoughtful. Below you will find a page dedicated solely for you reflection and thoughts so far.

Reflections

_____

Chapter 3 - The Home Stretch
Days 16 Through 21

Day 16

"Whoever would foster love covers over an offense, but whoever repeats the matter separates close friends."

The letter... This passage is a testament on how the power of love can cover any offense and the importance of allowing love to wash away hurts and pains experienced throughout the marriage.

Honey Bear,

As a married couple we have the distinct pleasure of sharing our lives together, however, this also means we see each other's faults. We will encounter problems that will make us upset and/or cause undue hurt and pain. I am learning that dwelling on the situation will only serve to cause strife between us. I am beginning to recognize the enemy and the doors/ traps he tries to open in marriage. I am learning to forgive faster and allow time for personal growth. I love you today, through all your faults and idiosyncrasies. I pray for patience, understanding and the ability to look past your imperfections and see you as God does. I will forgive not only you but myself for not being perfect. I will strive to be more like Christ and cover your offenses, other than holding them as a weapon for later...I will press towards the mark, and forgive you and me when we fall short.

Love always,

Your wife

Now it's your turn, you will find a work page to help you on your journey!

Love Letters to My Husband

Day 16

Scripture: Proverbs 17:9

NIV: Whoever would foster love covers over an offense, but whoever repeats the matter separates close friends.

Focus: It's your turn, it's important to let the Holy Spirit lead. What will you focus on?

_____
_____
_____
_____
_____
_____
_____
_____
_____
_____
_____

Use the above to write your letter. Remember that you are telling your husband what you will do according to the scriptures, not what he needs to do for you! This can be difficult but the exercise is in you finding your place in the relationship.

Next... Discuss the scripture with your spouse during the day or at night (basically your free quiet time together, please make time this is important). Also ask for his reflection as to his role. What can he do to follow the scripture towards you?

What was the outcome?

_____
_____
_____
_____
_____

Time to find your finishing power, don't stop short. You need to complete the process!

Day 17

"And he passed in front of Moses, proclaiming, "The LORD, the LORD, the compassionate and gracious God, slow to anger, abounding in love and faithfulness."

The letter... I really focused on faithfulness in this passage, it is my opinion that love and faithfulness flow together. What faithfulness means to me is the ability to love someone so much that you choose to follow, submit, and give them your all.

Dear Heart,

I was thinking back to the Bible about Ruth and how she left everything to follow her mother in law, she said where you go, I will go , let your God be my God and your people my people. It took great faith for her to leave everything behind and move forward to a land that was not familiar to her. That is a testament to the faithfulness of God to keep his promises. I love you babe and I will be faithful to you, I will do what I need to do, inside the will of God, to make sure our marriage is successful. We are a family. We are the primary unit. I will follow you as you follow Christ.

I love you,

Your wife

Now it's your turn, you will find a work page to help you on your journey!

Love Letters to My Husband

Day 17

Scripture: Exodus 34:6

NIV: And he passed in front of Moses, proclaiming, "The LORD, the LORD, the compassionate and gracious God, slow to anger, abounding in love and faithfulness.

Focus: I choose the word faithfulness, but you can look to the scripture and find your own focus to your spouse. Let the Holy Spirit lead and watch a miracle happen.

_____
_____
_____
_____
_____
_____
_____
_____
_____
_____
_____

Use the above to write your letter. Remember that you are telling your husband what you will do according to the scriptures, not what he needs to do for you! This can be difficult but the exercise is in you finding your place in the relationship.

Next... Discuss the scripture with your spouse during the day or at night (basically your free quiet time together, please make time this is important). Also ask for his reflection as to his role. What can he do to follow the scripture towards you? What was the outcome?

_____
_____
_____
_____
_____

Write down the things you would like to see in your marriage, keep a small journal or even a note, as a reminder of your goals.

Love Letters to My Husband

"Pray for the peace of Jerusalem: "May those who love you be secure.""

The letter... There is security in the love of God. We can rest assure that God loves us, look at His actions, and His grace, not only did He die for us. He is continually willing to forgive us. The Bible says noting can separate us from the love of Jesus. So my focus is on the security of God's love.

Dear Heart,

I hope and pray that in our young marital journey, you can feel secure in my love for you. I am so happy that God has brought us together. I waited a long time for my Boaz to come and now that I have you, I am on a quest to learn to love you as God does. I want the God in me to fall totally in love with the God in you, so when these bodies change, attitudes flair, tempers rise, and time passes it will not affect the love I have for you. I want to love you past the superficial to the spiritual being that is within you, so you will always be secure in my love.

I love you,

Your wife

Now it's your turn, you will find a work page to help you on your journey!

Love Letters to My Husband

Day 18

Scripture: Psalms 122:6

NIV: Pray for the peace of Jerusalem: "May those who love you be secure.

Focus: What will you focus on? You can choose my focus, but it's better to pray for your own.

_____
_____
_____
_____
_____
_____
_____
_____
_____
_____
_____
_____

Use the above to write your letter. Remember that you are telling your husband what you will do according to the scriptures, not what he needs to do for you! This can be difficult but the exercise is in you finding your place in the relationship.

Next... Discuss the scripture with your spouse during the day or at night (basically your free quiet time together, please make time this is important). Also ask for his reflection as to his role. What can he do to follow the scripture towards you?

What was the outcome?

_____
_____
_____
_____
_____

Write the vision and make it plain, are you keeping a log of what you want to see in your marriage? Declare it every day.

Love Letters to My Husband

Day 19

> "Let him lead me to the banquet hall, and let his banner over me be love."

The letter... The focus of this scripture for me was simple. The banner of love, wow this speaks to me about how God's love covers me at all times.

My heart,

Baby I know that you love me, and just knowing that your banner over me is love, allows me to go farther than I thought possible. The support that you give me allows me to be everything that God called me to be. I promise to strive to place a banner of love over you every day. I want you to see and feel that my love covers you. I pray that it allows you the freedom to be who you are in Christ, to make you a better father, husband and overall man. I pray that my banner will help you to conquer things that you never thought you could do. Thank you for loving me, and may God continue to spread his banner of love over us.

I love you,

wifey

Now it's your turn, you will find a work page to help you on your journey!

Love Letters to My Husband

Day 19

Scripture: Song of Songs 2:4

NIV: Let him lead me to the banquet hall, and let his banner over me be love.

Focus: What will you focus on? Let the Holy Spirit guide you. This will be beneficial to your marriage.

_____
_____
_____
_____
_____
_____
_____
_____
_____
_____
_____
_____

Use the above space to write your letter. Remember that you are telling your husband what you will do according to the scriptures, not what he needs to do for you! This can be difficult but the exercise is in you finding your place in the relationship.

Next... Discuss the scripture with your spouse during the day or at night (basically your free quiet time together, please make time this is important). Also ask for his reflection as to his role. What can he do to follow the scripture towards you?

What was the outcome?

_____
_____
_____
_____
_____

Is God the focus of your marriage? We always want to check our motives, make sure that what you want for your marriage is what God wants.

Day 20

"If I speak in the tongues of men or of angels, but do not have love, I am only a resounding gong or a clanging cymbal. [2]If I have the gift of prophecy and can fathom all mysteries and all knowledge, and if I have a faith that can move mountains, but do not have love, I am nothing. [3]If I give all I possess to the poor and give over my body to hardship that I may boast, but do not have love, I gain nothing."

The letter... I love this very familiar passage of scripture, it tells of all the good works that you can do in the name of Christ, but without love it's for naught.

> *Honey Bear,*
>
> *Though God has blessed me with the gift of prophecy, if I can't love my husband it's all for nothing. Though I work tirelessly for the church and give to the poor, if I can't love my spouse it's nothing. Real love suffers long and is kind, I am willing to love you forever baby, and work on speaking to you with kind words. I will always speak the truth in love, for part of my assignment is to bring out the King in you. I will go through the storms with you. I will believe God with you and for you. I will encourage your dreams and most of all I will remember that charity starts at home. May God bless us with the same kind of love he has shown his children.*
>
> *Love,*
>
> *ME*

Now it's your turn, you will find a work page to help you on your journey!

Love Letters to My Husband

Day 20

Scripture: 1 Corinthians 13:1

NIV: If I speak in the tongues[a] of men or of angels, but do not have love, I am only a resounding gong or a clanging cymbal. [2] If I have the gift of prophecy and can fathom all mysteries and all knowledge, and if I have a faith that can move mountains, but do not have love, I am nothing. [3] If I give all I possess to the poor and give over my body to hardship that I may boast, but do not have love, I gain nothing.

Focus: You can use my focus, but it's better to use your own. Let the Holy Spirit guide you in writing your letter.

_____

_____

_____

_____

_____

_____

_____

_____

_____

_____

Use the above to write your letter. Remember that you are telling your husband what you will do according to the scriptures, not what he needs to do for you! This can be difficult but the exercise is in you finding your place in the relationship.

Next... Discuss the scripture with your spouse during the day or at night (basically your free quiet time together, please make time this is important). Also ask for his reflection as to his role. What can he do to follow the scripture towards you?

What was the outcome?

_____

_____

_____

_____

_____

Keep visualizing your breakthrough; declare that you will have what God says you can have!

Day 21

"And over all these virtues put on love, which binds them all together in perfect unity."

The letter... This scripture is so profound to me because it says simply put on love. Emphasizing that love is something that we can choose to do and that choice is what binds us together.

Dear Heart,

I know now more than ever that we cannot be one without love. We have to put on love every day. I ask God to help me love you more, because love is a decision and when we took our vows I chose to love you. What is even more profound to me is that we can't have unity, not in our personal goals, marriage or life without love. It is the glue that helps our marriage work. For our children to be whole and for our relationships to function properly, we need to be bound together in love. Love unifies our life, so baby I am putting on love, every day, because it is more important for us to be unified and on one accord more than anything else, we have great purpose to fulfill for God and I thank him for showing me how to love you.

Now it's your turn, you will find a work page to help you on your journey!

Love Letters to My Husband

Day 21

Scripture: Colossians 3:14

NIV: And over all these virtues put on love, which binds them all together in perfect unity.

Focus: What will you take from this passage of scripture, a word, a phrase or a thought? Let the Holy Spirit lead, you can't go wrong.

_____
_____
_____
_____
_____
_____
_____
_____
_____
_____
_____

Use the above to write your letter. Remember that you are telling your husband what you will do according to the scriptures, not what he needs to do for you! This can be difficult but the exercise is in you finding your place in the relationship.

Next... Discuss the scripture with your spouse during the day or at night (basically your free quiet time together, please make time this is important). Also ask for his reflection as to his role. What can he do to follow the scripture towards you?

What was the outcome?

_____
_____
_____
_____
_____

Your perseverance will pay off! You are making strides in the natural but even more in the spirit. Keep going, don't quit!

Love Letters to My Husband

Thoughts for Week 3

This week I was feeling – Determined

I was feeling determined, that I could really see actual changes in our relationship, My Husband express to me, that he really had no idea I felt this deeply for him, surprised me , I thought why would I marry you if I didn't , but I guess he's not a mind reader. So happy that he is really beginning to see I'm on team Hicks.

How do you feel after this week?

_____

_____

_____

_____

_____

_____

_____

_____

_____

_____

_____

_____

_____

_____

_____

_____

_____

_____

_____

_____

_____

Chapter 4 - Sweet Success
Days 22 Through 30

Day 22

"For God so loved the world that he gave his one and only Son, that whoever believes in him shall not perish but have eternal life."

The letter...This scripture is a testament to God's love for the world and his redemptive power.

Dear Heart,

In God's infinite wisdom and with His love for the mankind, He knew that He would have to redeem us back to Himself. The shedding of an animal's blood was not powerful enough to return His creation back to Him. He knew the perfect sacrifice was His son. He freely gave salvation to the Jew and Gentile, wow, so glad we are allowed to reign with Him. So today as I think about God's redemptive power, His love, and not being a respecter of persons. I say to you, no matter what comes our way, I ask God to allow me to love the total man in you. That He will give me the grace to love you through your faults and that He will allow the love I have for you to overshadow all your imperfections. That today I will fall in love with the total man, and see your weaknesses no more. That He lets me see His sons blood covering you instead; pray that the same need to cover us, our sin, our fault, and imperfections, is the same yearning he gives to me during the trials of our marriage. I thank God for you, and plan on seeing this marriage through to the end. God will give me the grace and loving eyes I need to persevere.

Now it's your turn, you will find a work page to help you on your journey!

Day 22

Scripture: John 3:16

NIV: For God so loved the world that he gave his one and only Son, that whoever believes in him shall not perish but have eternal life.

Focus: You may use my focus, or you may choose one for yourself. Remember let God lead.

_____
_____
_____
_____
_____
_____
_____
_____
_____
_____
_____

Use the above to write your letter. Remember that you are telling your husband what you will do according to the scriptures, not what he needs to do for you! This can be difficult but the exercise is in you finding your place in the relationship.

Next... Discuss the scripture with your spouse during the day or at night (basically your free quiet time together, please make time this is important). Also ask for his reflection as to his role. What can he do to follow the scripture towards you?

What was the outcome?

_____
_____
_____
_____
_____

See yourself finishing this assignment. Don't give up! It's important to endure to the end!

Day 23

"There is no fear in love. But perfect love drives out fear, because fear has to do with punishment. The one who fears is not made perfect in love."

The letter...The focus for me is FEAR, we do so many things because of fear, and this makes me think of how secure we can be in God because of his love. I can only help my mate to feel secure in my own love for him.

Sweetie,

Thank God for love, and thank you for loving me. I don't fear that our love will fail, but I must repent to you and ask for forgiveness if I have ever made you feel as though I would leave you, at any time. I want our love to be without fear. I want us to be secure in our love for each other, and I know you need to feel secure in our marriage. I don't want you to have any doubts, so it is my prayer that God perfect the love in our marriage, so that it cast out all anxiety in our new marriage.

Now it's your turn, you will find a work page to help you on your journey!

Love Letters to My Husband

Day 23

Scripture: 1 John 4:18

NIV: There is no fear in love. But perfect love drives out fear, because fear has to do with punishment. The one who fears is not made perfect in love.

Focus: You may use my focus, or you may choose one for yourself. Remember let God lead.

_____
_____
_____
_____
_____
_____
_____
_____
_____
_____
_____
_____

Use the above to write your letter. Remember that you are telling your husband what you will do according to the scriptures, not what he needs to do for you! This can be difficult but the exercise is in you finding your place in the relationship.

Next... Discuss the scripture with your spouse during the day or at night (basically your free quiet time together, please make time this is important). Also ask for his reflection as to his role. What can he do to follow the scripture towards you?

What was the outcome?

_____
_____
_____
_____
_____
_____

Please note any changes that you see taking place and celebrate the small as well as any big changes.

Love Letters to My Husband

" Love the Lord *your God with all your heart and with all your soul and with all your strength."*

The letter... The only thing that should come before the love of my husband is the love I have for my God. In this scripture it gives so much insight into the way I am supposed to love you. In my pursuit to love God, I must also love the God in you.

My Love,

So, I was thinking how can I love my husband with all my heart, soul and might, (the same way I love God)? With God, I pray to Him and this leads me to talk to Him daily. So, when I think about my Husband, I will pray for you and spend time with you daily, I express my secret places to God, and so to my husband I will make you my best friend and trust you with my secrets. I believe and have faith in God, so I will believe in you, have faith with you and stand by you. I let nothing separate me from God, so I will put you in your rightful place in my life, I will build you up not tear you down, I will fight for our marriage, I won't let anyone or anything come between us.

Love you always,

Wifey

Now it's your turn, you will find a work page to help you on your journey!

Love Letters to My Husband

Day 24

Scripture: Deuteronomy 6:5

NIV: Love the LORD your God with all your heart and with all your soul and with all your strength.

Focus: You may use my focus, or you may choose one for yourself. Remember to let God lead.

_____
_____
_____
_____
_____
_____
_____
_____
_____
_____
_____
_____

Use the above to write your letter. Remember that you are telling your husband what you will do according to the scriptures, not what he needs to do for you! This can be difficult but the exercise is in you finding your place in the relationship.

Next... Discuss the scripture with your spouse during the day or at night (basically your free quiet time together, please make time this is important). Also ask for his reflection as to his role. What can he do to follow the scripture towards you?

What was the outcome?

_____
_____
_____
_____
_____

Please continue to see yourself, accomplishing your marital goals, keep your time with your spouse each night to discuss your letter.

Day 25

"Dear children, let us not love with words or speech but with actions and in truth."

The letter... Our actions are important. God shows us His love through actions. He gave His very life for us, He will answer our prayers, and He listens to our every need and is just to answer our every concern. So today I realize that love is an action.

> *My Love,*
>
> *I was thinking how can I show my love for you? Love is and action, and so I choose to spend time with you, talking and sharing life's ups and downs. I will give you the attention you need and deserve. I will ask you the important question "how do I make you feel loved?" I promise to pray and let God lead me in opening my heart to you, telling you my secrets and being truthful with you always. My prayer today is to put love in action and make you feel the love.*
>
> *Love you always,*
>
> *Wifey*

Now it's your turn, you will find a work page to help you on your journey!

Day 25

Scripture: 1 John 3:18

NIV: Dear children, let us not love with words or speech but with actions and in truth.

Focus: You may use my focus, or you may choose one for yourself. Remember to let God lead.

_____
_____
_____
_____
_____
_____
_____
_____
_____
_____
_____
_____

Use the above space to write your letter. Remember that you are telling your husband what you will do according to the scriptures, not what he needs to do for you! This can be difficult but the exercise is in you finding your place in the relationship.

Next... Discuss the scripture with your spouse during the day or at night (basically your free quiet time together, please make time this is important). Also ask for his reflection as to his role. What can he do to follow the scripture towards you?

What was the outcome?

_____
_____
_____
_____
_____

Your almost there, see yourself accomplishing your marital goals, keep your time with your spouse each night to discuss your letter.

Day 26

> *"But I say unto you, Love your enemies, bless them that curse you, do good to them that hate you, and pray for them which despitefully use you, and persecute you."*

The letter... Such a powerful scripture, it's a testament to how we should love those we are our enemies, and if we are to love our enemies this way how much more should we love those who God set in our life to be friends to us.

My love,

How I try so hard to love those who hurt you. I feel so strongly, and because you and I are one, when you hurt, I hurt and when you're in pain I feel it too. I ask God to help me love my enemies, and cover them with His love and forgiveness. It reminds me of my need to forgive and forget when we go through our own disagreements. The truth is, if I can pray for my enemies how, much more can I pray for the one my soul loveths? You are my best friend, confidant, husband, soul mate; I should have even greater compassion for you. I love you and it is my prayer that I am able to forgive and forget even those who hurt us and even more I am able to love you past the vicissitudes that we encounter.

Love you always,

Wifey

Yes I really wrote the word **vicissitudes**. A very prominent minister used it all the time, until I picked it up. Don't roll your eyes, I see you!

Now it's your turn, you will find a work page to help you on your journey!

Love Letters to My Husband

Day 26

Scripture: Matthew 5:44

KJV: But I say unto you, Love your enemies, bless them that curse you, do good to them that hate you, and pray for them which despitefully use you, and persecute you.

Focus: You may use my focus, or you may choose one for yourself. Remember to let God lead.

_____
_____
_____
_____
_____
_____
_____
_____
_____
_____
_____
_____

Use the above space to write your letter. Remember that you are telling your husband what you will do according to the scriptures, not what he needs to do for you! This can be difficult but the exercise is in you finding your place in the relationship.

Next... Discuss the scripture with your spouse during the day or at night (basically your free quiet time together, please make time this is important). Also ask for his reflection as to his role. What can he do to follow the scripture towards you?

What was the outcome?

_____
_____
_____
_____
_____

Please continue to declare over your marriage, and encourage your spouse to declare with you!

Love Letters to My Husband

" I love the LORD, because he hath heard my voice and my supplications."

The letter... In our time of trouble God will hear our pleas, for He can hear the issues of our heart. When we call on Him He will hear us and deliver us out of all our trouble, what a mighty God we serve. This is yet another reason we keep the hope and have faith in Him. This just shows me how to minister to my husband, who can't be strong all the time.

> *Dearest Husband,*
>
> *I am learning the importance of listening to you, not just listening, but actually hearing you. Oh how we give praise unto God for hearing us and responding in our time of need. Well it is my prayer that God almighty open the ears and eyes of our hearts, so that understanding will come in. I want to truly be best friends, may God help me hear you when you speak. May He help me understand you when you call on me. May He help me keep your confidences when shared; and may He allow me to really listen and hear you in times of anger, and help me put this flesh to the side so I can minister to you in your time of pain. Let my ministry be unto my husband. I want to be a true help meet to you.*
>
> *Love you always,*
>
> *Wifey*

Now it's your turn, you will find a work page to help you on your journey!

Love Letters to My Husband

Day 27

Scripture: Psalms 116:1

KJV: I love the LORD, because he hath heard my voice and my supplications.

Focus: You may use my focus, or you may choose one for yourself. Remember to let God lead.

_____
_____
_____
_____
_____
_____
_____
_____
_____
_____
_____
_____
_____

Use the above to write your letter. Remember that you are telling your husband what you will do according to the scriptures, not what he needs to do for you! This can be difficult but the exercise is in you finding your place in the relationship.

Next... Discuss the scripture with your spouse during the day or at night (basically your free quiet time together, please make time this is important). Also ask for his reflection as to his role. What can he do to follow the scripture towards you?

What was the outcome?

_____
_____
_____
_____
_____

Continue declaring God's vision over your marriage. It is more effective if you and your spouse do this together.

Love Letters to My Husband

"*Whoever does not love does not know God, because God is love.*"

The letter... To me this verse is so self-explanatory, that I am going to use it just as it is.

My love,

Short letter today my love, because I really feel the message is simple, we have to love God, and if we have no love for God, we cannot love each other. I'm so glad that we have gone through this exercise, because it teaching us how to love Him and by loving Him, how to love each other. I am happy that when we met the spirit of God was already in you, because even in my inability to love you right all the time, it dwells in both our hearts. Praise God that He is teaching me how to love you.

Love you always,

Wifey

Now it's your turn, you will find a work page to help you on your journey!

Day 28

Scripture: 1 John 4:8

NIV: For this reason a man will leave his father and mother and be united to his wife, and they will become one flesh.

Focus: You may use my focus, or you may choose one for yourself. Remember to let God lead.

_____
_____
_____
_____
_____
_____
_____
_____
_____
_____
_____
_____

Use the above space to write your letter. Remember that you are telling your husband what you will do according to the scriptures, not what he needs to do for you! This can be difficult but the exercise is in you finding your place in the relationship.

Next... Discuss the scripture with your spouse during the day or at night (basically your free quiet time together, please make time this is important). Also ask for his reflection as to his role. What can he do to follow the scripture towards you?

What was the outcome?

_____
_____
_____
_____
_____

Please continue to declare God's word over your marriage, visualize it, and see it as a reality.

Thoughts for Week 4

This week I was feeling –grateful

This week I am feeling totally grateful for this process. God truly made a difference in our marriage. It was a hard process to complete, and I wanted to give up a few times along the way, but God really taught me a lot about myself. Man we are walking in peace, and that makes me smile. We are even on one accord in regards to our son. Feeling so happy and in love again. I feel like singing God has smiled on me. I guess I won't have to exact revenge on him after all.

How do you feel after this week?

_____

_____

_____

_____

_____

_____

_____

_____

_____

_____

_____

_____

_____

_____

_____

_____

Love Letters to My Husband

" This is love: not that we loved God, but that he loved us and sent his Son as an atoning sacrifice for our sins."

The letter... This is a particularly inspiring passage to me; it tells of God's love for us, not that we loved Him, but that He first loved us. This is my focus today. God loved us, not the other way around.

> *My love,*
>
> *I remember you saying at one point that love is a choice. I was never entirely sure that I agreed with that statement, but now I see that in some respects it is a choice. However, like many other things, there is a prerequisite to making that choice; you have to have the love of God in you first. It makes me think back to when I heard people say that they just fell out of love , that to me is cop out. God never required anything for us to receive His love. He loves us, whether we accept His love or not. It was His own love that saved us, even when we despised Him. So if I get to the point where I feel I just don't like you today (I pray that doesn't happen) I remember that loves does not require another person's actions to revive it. It just takes one of us to show God's true love to overcome any obstacle sent by the enemy. May God cover us in His blood and keep us surrounded by His love.*
>
> *Love you always,*
>
> *Wifey*

Now it's your turn, you will find a work page to help you on your journey!

Love Letters to My Husband

Day 29

Scripture: 1 John 4:10

NIV: This is love: not that we loved God, but that he loved us and sent his Son as an atoning sacrifice for our sins.

Focus: You may use my focus, or you may choose one for yourself. Remember to let God lead.

_____
_____
_____
_____
_____
_____
_____
_____
_____
_____
_____

Use the above to write your letter. Remember that you are telling your husband what you will do according to the scriptures, not what he needs to do for you! This can be difficult but the exercise is in you finding your place in the relationship.

Next... Discuss the scripture with your spouse during the day or at night (basically your free quiet time together, please make time this is important). Also ask for his reflection as to his role. What can he do to follow the scripture towards you?

What was the outcome?

_____
_____
_____
_____
_____

What changes have you noticed? Write down, all changes to this point, you will need them for day 30.

Love Letters to My Husband

" Then they can urge the younger women to love their husbands and children, ⁵to be self-controlled and pure, to be busy at home, to be kind, and to be subject to their husbands, so that no one will malign the word of God."

The letter... I am so happy that I have a mother and father who have set a good example and taught me how to love my husband and they accomplished this by being living examples. I thank God that for being the ultimate teacher and the authority on how to love each other.

> *My love,*
>
> *The verse 5 speaks about being obedient to your husband. This has not always been easy, but when I see you submitted to God, I know that you would not try to take advantage of your position or authority over the family. Being a young woman in marriage and becoming a new mother all at the same time has been certainly a learning process. I am learning daily what it is to be a good wife and mother. For so long I have been single, caring only for myself and the things of God. I thank God He is teaching me to love you, to be obedient, and to be a good wife and mother. I love you and I pray that we continue to grow in the things of God, that our home life is pleasing to God, and that we will be an example of others to follow. It is my sincere desire to be a Titus type of woman.*
>
> *Love you always,*
>
> *Wifey*

Now it's your turn, you will find a work page to help you on your journey!

Love Letters to My Husband

Day 30

Scripture: Titus 2:4

NIV: Then they can urge the younger women to love their husbands and children, [5] to be self-controlled and pure, to be busy at home, to be kind, and to be subject to their husbands, so that no one will malign the word of God.

Focus: Write your own letter and be honest about your feelings; this will help you connect on a greater level.

_____
_____
_____
_____
_____
_____
_____
_____
_____
_____
_____

Use the above to write your letter. Remember that you are telling your husband what you will do according to the scriptures, not what he needs to do for you! This can be difficult but the exercise is in you finding your place in the relationship.

Next... Discuss the scripture with your spouse during the day or at night (basically your free quiet time together, please make time this is important). Also ask for his reflection as to his role. What can he do to follow the scripture towards you?

What was the outcome?

_____
_____
_____
_____
_____

Day 30! You made it! Now take what changed in your marriage and discuss why you think it changed, and continue on the journey to a new life, a new marriage and new love. ONE LOVE.

Conclusion

My marriage has not been perfect, but it has been so much better, we have learned to communicate, we have learned God's model for marriage through his love and commitment to us and that has been the greatest single factor to bring about change in our Union. We are happier, our family has much more peace and stability and I'm so carefully about asking God to "get" him, now I ask God to fix us. We are still learning, we are still growing, and the growing pains have not stopped, but we have a working model to live by, and it has made all the difference in the world. Have we faced challenges since this 30 day experience? Of course, but more than anything we have learned there is no mountain that we cannot conquer, there is no ocean that is too wide, as long as we lean on God through it all.

Our Declaration for Your Marriage

We would like to take the time to make a declaration over your marriage. We declare that God will heal, restore and renew your marriage. We declare that where there are weaknesses he will make them strong. While reading this book you are being restored and delivered from every trap that the enemy has set against your union; that you are walking in divine commitment to each other and that communication lines are open. We declare that God is mending broken hearts and frustrated spirits; that the enemy is being rebuked from your life and ungodly relationships are being torn down. We declare that that your affections are for one another and the fruits of the spirit are being birthed in your lives. We declare that God is the head of your union and that any thought that rises against your oneness is being made low. May God bless and keep you and may your marriage. May your marriage flourish and be enriched. May the passion never leave and may the flames of God's love perpetually be kindled in your life.

Appendix A: Declarations

1. Today Lord I declare that no weapon formed against our marriage shall prosper, we close every door that the enemy has opened or is trying to open in our marriage, and we declare that we are hedged in with protection on all sides and the blood of Jesus Is covering us each day.

2. Lord we thank you that when we took our vows, that we were united to not only one another but by your covenant. We thank you that a three strand cord is not easily broken, therefore we declare that we are unified, in the mind, body and spirit, we are walking on one accord, we are unified and in sync with each other, we thank you that we are truly walking in oneness.

3. Lord we thank you that we are not quick to anger, we thank you that, patience is having its perfection work in us and we walk with that same even temperance toward one another. We are seeing each other the way that you see us, and were able to be patient through the process.

4. Lord we declare that we only have eyes for each other, that are affections and desires cannot be stolen away, because they are based on your word that we are one, and we declare that anything that will steals these affections and desires will be removed in the name of Jesus. We declare that our love for each other is stronger and burns hotter each day, and we are walking in supernatural love for each other.

5. Lord we declare that we are operating in Godly wisdom, that we are seeking out God's purpose and plan for our lives, that we are in the divine will of God and any motives , agenda's or plans that are not of you are thwarted and we cancel every attack on our ability to conform to the will of God.

6. We declare by the power of Jesus Christ that no corrupt communication shall proceed from our mouths, that our words will be tempered by the fruits of the spirit, we will speak life over each other, and rebuke and words of death, defeat and destruction in Jesus name.

Appendix B: Love Level Quiz

1. How is your hearing?

    1.) Ear Plugs   2) Barely Listening   3.) Half Listening   4.) Active Listening

2. How is your vision?

    1.) Blurry /fuzzy   2.) Rolling your eye   3.) Squinting   4.) Seeing Straight

3. How is your neck?

    1.) Rigid   2.) Moving in a Circular Pattern   3.) Slightly Tensed   4.) Relaxed

4. What is your voice inflection?

    1.) Nonexistent   2.) High Pitched   3.) A Little Vibrato   4.) Maya Angelou

5. How are your words?

    1.) Piercing   2.) Sarcastic   3.) Patronizing   4.) Dripping with Honey

Total your points and see where you fall

1-7 … ***In Need of Prayer…*** you are running on empty (humpty dumpty fell off the wall), so I'm going to say to you more prayer more power, little prayer little power. Some come out only by fasting and praying, I need you to make sure you're doing both!

7-13… ***Fence Straddler…*** you are not sure how you feel (alter ego?) so I'm going to say to you push until something happens, take a stance and stay with it. Be ye hot or cold, because too much fence jumping is bad for your health.

13-20 … ***In the Press…*** you are pressing your way (hallelujah chorus, love is in the air) so I'm going to say to you fight the good fight of faith and stay the course, you are on the road to success. They that wait on the lord shall renew their strength.

Made in the USA
Columbia, SC
27 April 2022

59563128R00050